The Bird and the Bear

First Day at Pine Forest School

Steve "Dr. Bird" Birchak

To the Wood family,
be a good friend!
Steve "Dr. Bird" Birchak

Illustrations by Jeanne Benas

Royal Fireworks Press
Unionville, New York

Royal Fireworks Press
P.O. Box 399
41 First Avenue
Unionville, NY 10988-0399
(845) 726-4444
fax: (845) 726-3824
email: mail@rfwp.com
website: rfwp.com

ISBN: 978-0 89824-324-6

Publisher: Dr. T.M. Kemnitz
Editor: Jennifer Ault
Book designer: Christopher Tice
Cover designer: Kerri Ann Ruhl

Printed and bound in Unionville, New York, on acid-free paper using vegetable-based inks at the Royal Fireworks facility.

27o17 ps

Dedication

This book is dedicated to all the children who have had the courage to help other children, and to all the children who, like me, gained new courage because they had a friend who helped them.

This book is based on my life. I was encouraged for years to turn my experience into a children's book. My nickname was Birdie, and I befriended the Bear (Rick "the Bear" Behrendsen).

When I speak to parents and kids about bullying, I always share my real-life story of "The Bird and the Bear."

– Steve "Dr. Bird" Birchak

"Birdie!" Momma Bird called. "Come down and get some breakfast, or you'll be late for school."

Birdie pulled up the covers. He had never been to Pine Forest School.

Birdie hopped down the branches. "Mom, I don't want to go to school. I don't know anyone there, and I'm scared!"

Momma Bird chirped, "Don't worry, Birdie. All the animals go to Pine Forest School. It's where they learn wonderful things, and learning can be fun!"

But Birdie wanted to stay home.

Momma Bird insisted, so Birdie started walking to the school. He saw Chippy, Racky, and Skunker. They already had friends. Birdie had none.

Suddenly Birdie felt a paw on his back. Someone pulled his feathers. "Ow!" said Birdie. He looked up and saw an animal he had never seen before.

"What's your problem, little bird? Can't you have a little fun?" the animal asked. The other animals laughed.

Bunny tried to help. She said, "Don't worry about Badger, Foxy, and Rat. They are mean to lots of animals."

When Birdie got to school, he sat down at a desk. He was so small that he couldn't see over the top of it. He heard some of the animals laugh.

"Who let in the tiny bird?"

"Hey little birdie, where's your nest?"

"Why don't you grow some bigger feathers so you can fly?"

"Animals, animals!" the teacher called out. "Pay attention! My name is Ms. Owl. In my class, we do not laugh at each other; we help each other." Ms. Owl handed Birdie a pillow to sit on.

"Let's introduce ourselves to our fellow animals," Ms. Owl said.

Birdie saw animals he had never seen before.

"Hi! I'm Caribou. My friends call me Boo."

"I'm Frogger."

"I'm Beaver."

There were so many different animals in the forest. Some animals were small, like Otter and Ducky, but none of them were as small as Birdie.

When it was Birdie's turn, he chirped, "My name is Birdie!"

Rat laughed, "He's so tiny he might get stepped on!"

Birdie felt sad.

Some animals laughed, but Birdie noticed that one animal was not laughing. He was big and covered with fur. He quietly sat alone and didn't seem to have any friends either.

Later Birdie went to lunch. The lunch lady, Mrs. Hawkey, yelled, "Who's holding up this line! What do you want? Stand up!"

Birdie was already standing up! Mrs. Hawkey couldn't see him.

After lunch Birdie went to gym class. All of the animals came together in a big clearing for gym. Mr. Mustang blew his whistle and had the animals line up in alphabetical order. He called out, “Badger! Bear! Birdie! Chippy!”

Birdie stood in line next to the biggest animal he had ever seen. This animal was tall and wide. He must have weighed at least five hundred pounds more than Birdie!

"Oh my," Birdie said, "he's as big as a monster!"

The big animal turned toward him and said, "Hey! Who are you?"

Birdie was so scared he couldn't talk!

In a deep voice, the big animal said again, “Hey, who are you?”

“I’m… I’m… I’m Birdie.” Birdie watched in fear as a great big paw came toward him.

“Nice to meet you! My name is Bear!”

Birdie relaxed, reached out with his wing, and touched the big paw. Bear gave him a gentle high five!

“Birdie, are you new at school?” Bear asked him.

“Yes, it’s my first day,” Birdie replied.

“Me too!” said Bear. “Birdie, are you having fun at school?”

“Oh Bear, it’s not very fun,” Birdie said. “I don’t have any friends, and some of the animals are making fun of me!”

Bear put his huge arm around Birdie. “It’s okay, Birdie. You have a friend now because I’ll be your friend.”

Birdie smiled. He was so happy to have a new friend!

Mr. Mustang blew his whistle. "It's time for a game of acorn!" The animals cheered because they loved the acorn game. To score points, you had to throw a big acorn into a knothole in a tree.

"Animals! Animals! Get into teams!" said Mr. Mustang.

Badger, Foxy, and Rat formed a team without including any of the other animals. So Birdie, Bunny, Chippy, and Skunker formed their own team.

Mr. Mustang blew his whistle, and the game began. In the first play, Badger, Foxy, and Rat ran right over Birdie. They grabbed the acorn and threw it in the knothole. "One point for us!" yelled Rat.

The acorn was so big that Birdie could hardly hold it. He threw it to Bunny, but Badger knocked her to the ground and took it away! Foxy threw it into the knothole and hollered, "Another point for us!"

Soon Badger's team had six points, and Birdie's team had none!

After Badger's team scored again, Mr. Mustang stopped the game so that every animal could get a drink of water from the stream. Bear walked over to Birdie and said, "Birdie, no one noticed that I didn't get picked for a team, and now I don't have one. Can I be on your team?

"Yes, Bear!" said Birdie.

Bunny, Chippy, and Skunker all welcomed Bear.

"I have an idea," said Bear. "When we get the acorn, let's use some teamwork. We will throw it to each other, and when I get near the knothole, pass it to me! I'm tall, and I can score easily!" The animals agreed.

When the game started again, Birdie's team threw the acorn back and forth until Bear was near the knothole. Skunker threw it as high as he could, and Bear grabbed it out of the air and scored! Everyone cheered!

Birdie's team scored again and again and again. Soon the game was almost over. Badger's team had seven points, and Birdie's team had seven points. The score was tied!

Mr. Mustang blew his whistle and said, "Only ten seconds left in the game!" Bear held the acorn in his paws, but he couldn't get close to the knothole because the other animals surrounded him.

Suddenly he had an idea. Bear held the acorn over his head and yelled, "Fly, Birdie, fly!"

Birdie flapped his wings as hard as he could and flew toward the knothole.

Bear threw the acorn to Birdie. Birdie grabbed it in his claws and dropped it into the knothole just as Mr. Mustang blew his whistle and said, "Time's up! The game is over!"

Birdie, Bear, Bunny, Chippy, and Skunker cheered! They had won the game!

"Hooray!" they yelled. "Hooray!"

As the animals walked to their next class, Bear picked up Birdie and put him on his shoulder. "Birdie," he said, "I'm so glad that you are my new friend."

Birdie said, "Bear, I'm so glad that you are my new friend too. I think I'm going to like Pine Forest School."

For the rest of the day, Birdie and Bear were together. They sat next to each other in math class as they counted pine cones.

They sang together in Mr. Frog's music class. Birdie chirped and Bear roared.

Birdie was happy. There were so many nice animals at school. The kindest animal was Bear. He was gentle, helpful, and a good friend.

Birdie couldn't wait to get home and tell Momma Bird that she was right! School is fun, and it's even better when you have a good friend!

Questions for children:

1. Birdie was afraid to go to his first day of school. Have you ever been afraid to try something new?
    a. What did you do?
    b. How did it turn out?
2. Have you ever noticed another boy or girl who was afraid of something new?
    a. What did you do?
    b. What would happen if you talked to him or her or asked him or her to be your friend?
3. Has anyone ever been mean to you? How did it feel?
4. Have you ever been mean to someone? How do you think the other person felt?
5. Getting along with other boys and girls is important. What would happen if no one got along?
6. Birdie and Bear both felt alone and afraid when school started. Then they became friends. What's the best way to make a friend?

Questions for the adults who guide children:

1. Children see parents, teachers, and even the most influential people in our country (politicians, movie stars, reality stars) being cruel. How do you discuss this with children? How do you model how to discuss problems without being cruel, insulting, or degrading to other people?
2. What steps can you take to make your learning environment, home, or classroom a true community where trust and respect are displayed by all members?

Tips for getting along with others:

1. **Remember: You don't have to be perfect to get along with others.** You just have to recognize when you are feeling angry, unkind, or crabby. Accept no excuses in yourself, and commit to change.
2. **You don't have to agree with everyone, love everyone, or even like everyone.** You simply must commit to respecting people and keeping peace.
3. **Start with a goal of trying not to harm anyone**. Try to keep in mind what the Dalai Lama once said: "Our prime purpose in this life is to help others. And if you can't help them, at least don't hurt them."
4. **Own your attitude.** You cannot blame anyone for your attitude. You cannot say, "You make me crazy...," "You ruined my day...," "Look what you made me do...," "I'll start treating others well when they start treating me well...," etc.
5. **Remove all conditions for being a decent and kind person.** You cannot say, "As soon as this is over...," "As soon as I start feeling better...," "As soon as he....," "As soon as she...starts doing her job...arrives on time...agrees with me...acts the way I want her to...THEN I will start treating her kindly!" If you place conditions on when you will start being a decent person, you will never be a decent person.
6. **Try to see the good in others before you see the bad.**